The Best Pet for Me

Is a FISH
a Good Pet for Me?

Jason Brainard

PowerKiDS
press™

New York

Published in 2020 by The Rosen Publishing Group, Inc.
29 East 21st Street, New York, NY 10010

First Edition

Editor: Elizabeth Krajnik
Book Design: Rachel Rising

Photo Credits: Cover, p.1 Vangert/Shutterstock.com; cover, pp. 1, 3, 4, 6, 8, 10, 12, 14, 16, 18, 20, 22, 23, 24 (background) Anna_leni/Shutterstock.com; back cover, p. 3 Tawatchai Jaeng-im/Shutterstock.com; p. 4 0306PAT/Shutterstock. com; p. 5 Grigorii Pisotsckii/Shutterstock.com; p. 6 Karel Kralovec/Shutterstock.com; p. 7 Tatiana Gordievskaia/Shutterstock.com; p. 8 Lamyai/Shutterstock.com; p. 9 Inspired By Maps/Shutterstock.com; p. 10 photosync/Shutterstock.com; p. 11 bogonet/Shutterstock.com; pp. 12,15, 22 Mirko Rosenau/Shutterstock.com; p. 13 Susie Cushner/The Image Bank/Getty Images; p.14 CKP1001/Shutterstock.com; p. 17 SUPEE PURATO/Shutterstock.com; p. 18 showcake/Shutterstock.com; p. 19 hedgehog94/Shutterstock.com; p. 20 Monika Wisniewska/Shutterstock.com; p. 21 Suchart Boonyavech/Shutterstock.com.

Library of Congress Cataloging-in-Publication Data

Names: Brainard, Jason, author.
Title: Is a fish a good pet for me? / Jason Brainard.
Description: New York : PowerKids Press, [2020] | Series: The best pet for me
 | Includes index.
Identifiers: LCCN 2018050449| ISBN 9781725301047 (paperback) | ISBN
 9781725301061 (library bound) | ISBN 9781725301054 (6 pack)
Subjects: LCSH: Aquarium fishes-Juvenile literature. | Pets-Juvenile
 literature.
Classification: LCC SF457.25 .B73 2020 | DDC 639.34-dc23
LC record available at https://lccn.loc.gov/2018050449

Manufactured in the United States of America

CPSIA Compliance Information: Batch #CSPK19. For Further Information contact Rosen Publishing, New York, New York at 1-800-237-9932.

Contents

A Fish for a Pet?

Have you ever thought about getting a pet? Do you want one that doesn't get hair all over the house? Or do you want one that doesn't make a lot of noise? Do you want one that doesn't make messes? If you answered "yes" to these questions, a fish might be a good pet for you.

Fish can be some of the cheapest pets to care for. They can also be one of the easiest pets to care for. However, having a pet is still a big **responsibility**. If you think you're ready to get a pet fish, read on to find out what it takes to care for one.

Pet Report

There are more than 25,000 species, or kinds, of fish on Earth. Only about 2,000 species of fish can survive in a home aquarium.

Even though goldfish can handle many different conditions, they still need special care. Read up on what goldfish need to live well.

Different Kinds of Fish

Of the many species of fish that can survive in household aquariums, some species, such as the common goldfish, live in room-**temperature** fresh water. Others, such as the blue danio, live in fresh water that must be heated. Fish that need to live in heated water are known as **tropical** or subtropical fish.

Some fish need to live in salt water. Just like some freshwater fish, some species of saltwater fish also need to live in heated water. A clownfish is a tropical saltwater fish that needs water that's 78°Fahrenheit (25.5°Celsius) or a little warmer. Which type of fish do you think would fit your lifestyle best?

Pet Report

Many people choose to get a freshwater fish that lives in room-temperature water for their first pet fish. These fish often cost less and are easier to care for than other kinds of fish.

Tropical saltwater fish can cost a lot of money. Starting a saltwater tank for tropical fish may also require more supplies, which means spending even more money.

Fish Facts

What makes a fish a fish? Fish live in water. Instead of arms and legs, fish have a number of fins. Fish are cold blooded. This means their body temperature depends on the temperature of the water they live in. Fish have **backbones**. Many, but not all, fish have scales. Fish, unlike land animals, get **oxygen** by passing water through their **gills**.

Because your fish will live in an aquarium, you'll need to clean its tank often. Fish, just like all living things, create waste. If your fish's water becomes too dirty, your fish won't be able to breathe and may become unhealthy.

gills

Fish have lived on Earth for more than 480 million years!

Aquariums

The kind of aquarium you'll need depends on what type of fish you want to get. The size of your aquarium also depends on how many fish you have. The more fish you have, the more often you'll need to clean your aquarium. Some aquariums may have a cover, a **filter** that cleans the water, and a heater.

You should set your tank up about a week before you bring your new fish home. First, add about a pound (0.45 kg) of rinsed **gravel** to the tank for every gallon (3.8 L) of water. Then add some **decorations**, such as fake or real plants.

fake plant

Pet Report

Not all fish get along. If you want more than one fish, make sure the species are known to get along and can survive in the same kind of water.

Fish need enough room to swim to be healthy. The Humane Society of the United States says that first-time fish owners should get a 20-gallon (75.7 L) tank to start.

Healthy Fish

Besides needing clean water and room to swim, fish also need the right food to be healthy. The type of food your fish needs depends on what species of fish it is. Before you get your fish, you should look up which food is the best for it. However, the least expensive food likely isn't the best food for your fish.

The temperature of your fish's water is important for its health. If you have tropical fish, their water must be heated to the right temperature or they'll die. However, not all fish need heated water. Make sure your aquarium's water is the right temperature for your fish.

aquarium thermometer

Pet Report

You should never flush your fish down the toilet or dump it in a nearby body of water. Flushing fish can make your water unsafe and your fish probably isn't native to your area.

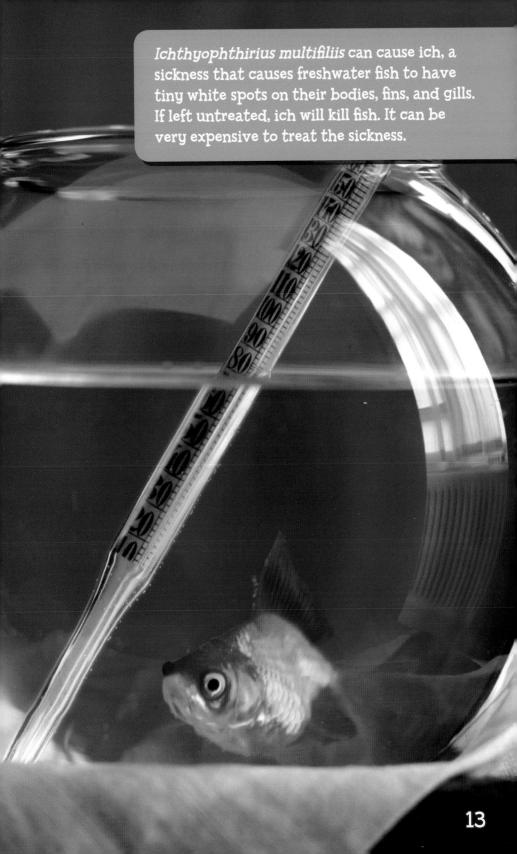

Ichthyophthirius multifiliis can cause ich, a sickness that causes freshwater fish to have tiny white spots on their bodies, fins, and gills. If left untreated, ich will kill fish. It can be very expensive to treat the sickness.

Feeding

In the wild, fish eat when they're hungry and when there's food around. That means your fish will probably eat whenever you feed it. For most fish, it doesn't really matter what time of day you feed them.

Most fish should be fed at least once a day. However, how often you should feed your fish depends on what kind of fish you have. If you feed your fish too often or too much, the extra food can make the water dirty. Remove extra food with a net. You should only feed your fish what it can eat in five minutes.

If you have different species of fish, you need to make sure each one is getting the right kind of food.

Cleaning Your Aquarium

How often you clean your aquarium depends on how many fish you have, what kind of fish you have, and how messy it is. Most aquariums should be cleaned at least once every two weeks.

The first step when cleaning your aquarium is to take your fish out and put them in a separate bowl. Clean the inside of the glass with an **algae** scrubber. Then, take out and scrub all the decorations with an algae scrubber. Next, clean the gravel with a water **siphon**. Clean the outside of the aquarium with special cleaner. Two weeks later, you should clean the filter.

Pet Report

A **chemical** called chlorine in tap water can make fish sick or kill them. Before getting a fish, you should make sure you have supplies to make your water safe.

If your fish tank gets too warm, gets too much sunlight, or has too many fish in it, algae may grow. If this happens, you may need a special sponge to clean the glass.

Buying Your Fish

Many large chain pet stores and small local pet stores sell fish. When buying a fish, it's important to ask questions. Ask what kind of fish it is, what type of water it needs, what other kinds of fish it gets along with, what type of food it eats, and how large it will grow to be.

You should always make sure the fish you're buying looks healthy. Healthy fish are lively and active. They have clear eyes, full stomachs, and well-shaped fins that don't show signs of harm. They should be breathing easily, look clean and colorful, and show that they're interested in eating.

Pet Report

Most saltwater fish sold in the United States are taken from the wild. Some are taken from the ocean even though there are laws against this. Many fish owners don't know this. You should think about this before buying a saltwater fish.

Buying your fish from the pet store is a good way to make sure you're getting the fish you want. Buying fish online can be tricky.

Benefits of Fish

All pets require time and effort—including fish. Fish don't need to be walked, can't scratch up your walls, and won't ruin your furniture. However, fish do need to have the right water, food, and companion fish.

Studies have shown that having an aquarium can lower people's blood pressure. Aquariums in dentist's offices help calm patients who are scared. One study even showed that people with **Alzheimer's disease** ate better and were livelier when there was an aquarium around. However, you might not need a real aquarium to see benefits. People who watch videos of fish with calming music also see some of the same benefits.

A small desk aquarium may help busy people relax.

What You'll Need

Fish: $3 to $12 each depending on species

Tank: $50 for a basic 20-gallon (75.7 L) tank

Gravel: $3 to $20 depending on kind and quantity

Live plants: $4 to $34 depending on kind and quantity

Decorations: $2 for a fake plant to $70 for a sunken battleship

Net: $2 to $5

Water Conditioner: $3 to $13 depending on type and size

Filter with Pump: $12 to $60 depending on size

Heater: $8 to $42 depending on size

Thermometer: $2 to $10 depending on type

Food: $4 to $14 depending on kind and quantity

Total Estimated Cost for Beginning Supplies:
$93 to $330

Glossary

algae: Simple plants that grow in or near water and have no leaves or stems. The singular is "alga."

Alzheimer's disease: A disease of the brain that causes people to slowly lose their memory and mental abilities.

backbone: The row of connected bones that go down the middle of the back and protect the spinal cord.

chemical: Matter that can be mixed with other matter to cause changes.

decoration: Something that is added to something else to make it prettier or nicer.

filter: A machine that removes impurities from something, such as water.

gill: The body part that animals such as fish use to breathe in water.

gravel: Small pieces of rock and pebbles larger than grains of sand.

oxygen: A chemical found in the air that has no color, taste, or smell, and that is necessary for life.

responsibility: The quality or state of being in charge of someone or something.

siphon: A bent pipe or tube through which a liquid can be drawn by air pressure up and over the edge of a container.

temperature: How hot or cold something is.

tropical: Relating to warm areas of Earth called the tropics.

Index

Websites

Due to the changing nature of Internet links, PowerKids Press has developed an online list of websites related to the subject of this book. This site is updated regularly. Please use this link to access the list: www.powerkidslinks.com/bpfm/fish